Whoops!

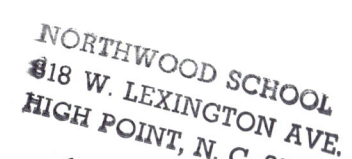

Written by Maureen Haselhurst

Illustrated by Mike Reed

Mom was fed up. She got mad when I made a sweet sticky mess with my green lemonade.

Then Dad bumped the car. He didn't take care.
He said, "Go tell Mom—do you think that we dare?"

Mom was fixing an old leaky pipe with some tape.
When she heard, she let go and the water escaped.

She yelled, "Get a mop! This is no time to mope. The whole house is soggy! I hope I can cope!"

We used Grandma's hat—it's a hat that I hate.
It made a good mop, but she got in a state.

My kid brother Tim didn't come home on time.
He fell into a pond and got covered in slime.

In his squelchy wet rags, he went into a rage.
It was then that the parrot got out of its cage.

The cat spat at the parrot—she spits out of spite.
Then the dog bit the cat—and that doggy can bite!

They all chased the fish—she's Min and she's mine.
Min waved a brave fin to say she was fine.

"Cut it out!" shouted Dad. "Pets should be cute."
They all snuggled down as I played on my flute.

Then Grandad came in with a kit for a kite,
with a wig-wagging tail in orange and white.

He had in his pocket a plan for a plane.
It was easy to make with some paper and cane.

We went into the yard and slid down the slide.
Grandad tore his best shirt, so we went back inside.

He made us the kite,
and he made us the plane—
they zoomed into the window
and crashed through the pane!

But no one got mad at the mess that we'd made.
We had a huge hug and drank green lemonade.